A Day On Crocus Hill With Sweetgrass

First Edition: Number 0274/ 2000

National Library of Canada Cataloguing in Publication

Williams Franzin, Sharon, 1948-
A day on Crocus Hill with Sweetgrass / Sharon Williams Franzin and
Firmin G. Michiels.

Includes bibliographical references.
ISBN 0-9732467-0-7

I. Michiels, Firmin G., 1930- II. Title.

PZ7.W657Da 2004   j813'.6   C2004-900638-X

First Edition

Published by Laughing Water Arts, Winnipeg, Manitoba, Canada

Printed and bound by
Friesens Corporation, One Printers Way, Altona, Manitoba, Canada, R0G 0B0

A Day On Crocus Hill

With

Sweetgrass

Sharon Williams Franzin
and
Firmin G. Michiels

Laughing Water Arts

In Honour Of The Creator:

"Chi Meegwetch", "Merci", "Thank You", for the GIFT OF LIFE.

To Our Parents,

Helena (Cnudde) and Robert Michiels,

Rosalia Maria (Tschurwald) and Joseph Williams

And

To All Our Relations:

"A crocus flower just for you,
To fill your heart with sunshine through."

🍁 National Anthem Of Canada 🍁

O Canada!
Our home and native land!
True patriot love
In all thy sons command.
With glowing hearts
We see thee rise,
The True North strong and free!
From far and wide,
O Canada,
We stand on guard for thee.
God keep our land
Glorious and free!
O Canada,
We stand on guard for thee.
O Canada,
We stand on guard for thee.

O Canada!
Terre de nos aïeux,
Ton front est ceint
De fleurons glorieux!
Car ton bras
Sait porter l'épée,
Il sait porter la croix!
Ton histoire
Est une épopée
Des plus brillants exploits.
Et ta valeur,
De foi trempée,
Protégera nos foyers
Et nos droits,
Protégera nos foyers
Et nos droits.

English Lyrics by Mr. Justice Robert Stanley Weir
French Lyrics by Sir Adolphe-Basile Routhier
Music by Calixa Lavallée

Preface

Author Sharon Williams Franzin felt an urgency to relate her story about Crocus Hill and of the creatures great and small that lived there. Her fervent desire to share her pleasures and experiences with children was a strong motivator for writing. Artist-naturalist, the author appeals to the young in spirit as she describes, in her unique philosophical manner, the interdependence of all living things.

Her reverence for the aging, her interest in mythology and devotion to the preservation of the environment are messages dispersed throughout the story. To portray cultural practices and beliefs as accurately as possible, the author conferred with knowledgeable Elders, thus adding a living component to the whole project.

Considering all the sounds and activities on Crocus Hill, there pervades an ambience of peace and tranquility. The whole occurrence results in a delightful, wholesome story.

Anne Smigel,
Educator

Author's Foreword

My parents were adventurous in spirit and loved Nature. While they pursued their dreams, I was immersed in the untamed north woods of Manitoba. There I learned to value life, to understand the fragility and strength of a human soul, to love the woods and lakes and to respect and survive the elements. As a youngster, I was known as "Papoose". My Elders guided me with patience, love and kindness, encouraging my curiosity and creative expression. Together, we lived in a three-room log cabin in a remote wilderness surrounded by Aboriginal (First Nations) Elders, rough trappers, wild-eyed prospectors, savvy guides, "men of good hearts" (missionary priests) and the "stripes" (Royal Canadian Mounted Police).

The community included a colourful array of immigrant adventure-seekers from around the world. The bounty of the environment north of the 54th Parallel instilled in me strong feelings of connection to the natural world. I listened to and was influenced by what Elders said, for they lived simply, toiling with courageous spirit in an effort to survive. Observing Nature, asking questions and discovering the good in "all creation" enriched my life.

Southwestern Manitoba is of particular significance to this story because Artist-photographer Firmin Michiels grew up on his parents' farm in the Tiger Hills (Blue Hills) area, among the Wild Prairie-Crocus flowers. As a youngster, he developed a love of Nature, especially the beauty of wildflowers. His interest in the natural world grew while he completed his post-secondary education. During those years, Michiels became acquainted with ardent naturalist Father Gerard De Ruyck. Together, they shared hobbies and enjoyed many field expeditions.

Through the years, co-author and photographer Firmin Michiels and I have shared countless discussions on all aspects of flora, fauna and astronomy. Michiel's years of studying Nature, as exemplified in outstanding photographic compositions, connect the real world to *A Day On Crocus Hill With Sweetgrass.*

Sweetgrass is a fictional character. The story is based on Aboriginal culture generally, without reference to any First Nation. However, the collective material used in the writing of this story is factual and includes information gleaned from spending many spring days, from sunrise to sunset, on several Manitoba Crocus Hills. Having visited many such hills over the years, my co-author and I decided to record the various wildlife activities and other natural phenomena that could be observed by spending one day on one Crocus Hill.

We hope that this story will teach tolerance of and respect for Nature because we all are joined ecologically in the "Circle of Life". People the world over traditionally venerate Nature in food, song, dance and folklore.

It is our wish that this book may serve as a teaching tool about plants, animals and elements of the Prairies, demonstrating how everything in our world is interdependent. A world-wide celebration of this interdependence is *International Earth Day*, commemorated on the Spring Equinox each year. We also encourage respect and admiration for the heritage of our indigenous peoples and their spirituality.

As you accompany Sweetgrass on this imaginary journey, may you learn to observe, experience and enjoy the many facets of the flora and fauna of our wild Prairies.

A sharing of minds, hearts and souls took *A Day On Crocus Hill With Sweetgrass* from a little seed into full bloom. We offer this story to you with all our love.

The Life And Spirit Of The Wild Prairie-Crocus

The Wild Prairie-Crocus represents the true spirit of First Nations peoples and pioneer settlers, exemplifying their many struggles to survive. The Prairie environment tested the stamina of these people who approached life with faith, hope and love in their hearts.

Aboriginal (First Nations) peoples attributed spirits to the Wild Prairie-Crocus flowers that covered the Prairie hills each spring. Therefore, it was appropriate that the Prairie-Crocus was chosen by the young children of Manitoba to become the Provincial Floral Emblem. The flower was assigned this status through Royal Assent on March 16, 1906. A special Crocus Day was established on that day each year to venerate and wear Nature's gift, the Wild Prairie-Crocus flower. However, we recommend that wildflowers be enjoyed in the wild and not be picked.

Colour Plates

		Page
PLATE 1.	THE WILD PRAIRIE-CROCUS, *ANEMONE PATENS*.	2
PLATE 2.	COMMON BEARBERRY (KINNIKINNICK), *ARCTOSTAPHYLOS UVA-URSI*.	3
PLATE 3.	LABRADOR-TEA, *LEDUM GROENLANDICUM*.	4
PLATE 4.	PITCHERPLANT, *SARRACENIA PURPUREA* (INSET: LEAF CUP).	5
PLATE 5.	WILD PRAIRIE-CROCUS CLUSTER.	7
PLATE 6.	CROCUS CUP.	8
PLATE 7.	LUMINOUS BUDDING CROCUSES.	9
PLATE 8.	BEES FORAGE FOR SWEET CROCUS NECTAR AND POLLEN IN EARLY SPRING.	11
PLATE 9.	OPEN CROCUSES REFLECT THE RADIANCE OF THE WARM SPRING SUN.	12
PLATE 10.	PRAIRIE BUTTERCUP, *RANUNCULUS RHOMBOIDEUS*.	14
PLATE 11.	THREE-FLOWERED AVENS, *GEUM TRIFLORUM* (INSET: SEED STAGE).	15
PLATE 12.	PURPLE CROCUS FLOWER GOBLET.	16
PLATE 13.	THE RARE WHITE COLOUR VARIATION OF THE WILD PRAIRIE-CROCUS.	17
PLATE 14.	A CLUSTER OF RARE WHITE WILD PRAIRIE-CROCUSES.	18
PLATE 15.	SEED STAGE OF THE WILD PRAIRIE-CROCUS.	19
PLATE 16.	UPPER LEFT: MARSH-MARIGOLD, *CALTHA PALUSTRIS*; LOWER LEFT: PRAIRIE SAGE, *ARTEMISIA LUDOVICIANA*; RIGHT: FIELD MINT, *MENTHA ARVENSIS*.	20
PLATE 17.	YELLOW LADY'S-SLIPPER, *CYPRIPEDIUM CALCEOLUS*.	21
PLATE 18.	LEFT: FLORETS OF SWEET GRASS, *HIEROCHLOË ODORATA*; RIGHT: PINK WINTERGREEN, *PYROLA ASARIFOLIA*.	22
PLATE 19.	PRINCE'S-PINE (WINTERGREEN), *CHIMAPHILA UMBELLATA*.	23
PLATE 20.	UPPER LEFT: WESTERN CANADA VIOLET, *VIOLA RUGULOSA*; UPPER RIGHT: COMMON BLUE-EYED GRASS, *SISYRINCHIUM MONTANUM*; BOTTOM: ARUM-LEAVED ARROWHEAD, *SAGITTARIA CUNEATA*.	24
PLATE 21.	BLUE FLAG, *IRIS VERSICOLOR*.	25
PLATE 22.	YELLOW POND-LILY, *NUPHAR VARIEGATUM*.	26
PLATE 23.	BEAKED HAZELNUT, *CORYLUS CORNUTA*; LEFT: FLOWER; RIGHT: TWINNED NUT.	27

Colour Plates Continued

Page

PLATE 24. GREAT HORNED OWL, *BUBO VIRGINIANUS*; STORY NAME: TIGER HILLS OWL.   28

PLATE 25. SASKATOON, *AMELANCHIER ALNIFOLIA*; LEFT: FLOWER; RIGHT: BERRY.   29

PLATE 26. WESTERN RED LILY, *LILIUM PHILADELPHICUM*.   30

PLATE 27. LONG-HEADED CONEFLOWER, *RATIBIDA COLUMNIFERA*.   31

PLATE 28. WESTERN WILD BERGAMOT, *MONARDA FISTULOSA*.   32

PLATE 29. FLODMAN'S THISTLE, *CIRSIUM FLODMANII*.   33

PLATE 30. UPPER LEFT: MARSH-MARIGOLD, *CALTHA PALUSTRIS*; UPPER RIGHT: SHINING ARNICA, *ARNICA FULGENS*; LOWER LEFT: GREAT-FLOWERED GAILLARDIA, *GAILLARDIA ARISTATA*; LOWER RIGHT: BLACK-EYED SUSAN, *RUDBECKIA HIRTA*.   34

PLATE 31. SCARLET PAINTBRUSH, *CASTILLEJA COCCINEA*.   35

PLATE 32. TOP: WILD CUCUMBER, *ECHINOCYSTIS LOBATA*; LEFT: COMMON HOP, *HUMULUS LUPULUS*; RIGHT: BUDS OF PRAIRIE ONION, *ALLIUM STELLATUM*.   36

PLATE 33. MEADOW BLAZINGSTAR, *LIATRIS LIGULISTYLIS*; LEFT: FLOWER; RIGHT: SEED STAGE.   37

PLATE 34. TOP: PRAIRIE ONION, *ALLIUM STELLATUM*; BOTTOM: YARROW, *ACHILLEA MILLEFOLIUM*.   38

PLATE 35. PURPLE CONEFLOWER, *ECHINACEA ANGUSTIFOLIA*.   39

PLATE 36. WILD PRAIRIE ROSE, *ROSA SPECIES* (INSET: ROSEHIPS; SEED STAGE).   40

PLATE 37. A SPIDER AND A BEE REST BRIEFLY ON A PRAIRIE-CROCUS FLOWER TO ABSORB WARMTH FROM THE SUN ON A CHILLY MORNING.   42

PLATE 38. WILD PRAIRIE-CROCUSES BEGIN TO CLOSE WITH THE SETTING OF THE SUN.   44

PLATE 39. A FEATHERY PRAIRIE-CROCUS SEED.   46

Colour Plates Continued

Page

PLATE **40.**   *Sweetgrass*, a denizen of the sky, journeys among the celestial star-flowers like the ephemeral Comet Hale-Bopp, shown here.   **47**

Notes

Common and Latin names of the flowers in the photographs were determined from two main references: *The Flora of Canada* by H.J. Scoggan. 1978. National Museum of Natural Sciences, National Museums of Canada, Ottawa, Canada. 1711p. and *Budd's Flora of the Canadian Prairie Provinces*, Revised Edition by J. Looman and K.F. Best. 1987. Research Branch, Agriculture Canada Publication 1662. 863p.

Geographical names were researched in *Geographical Names of Manitoba*, 2000. Manitoba Conservation. 323p. or from topographic maps.

Information on Comet Hale-Bopp was obtained from the NASA website: http://encke.jpl.nasa.gov/hale_bopp_info.html.

The Life Cycle Of The Wild Prairie-Crocus Flower, from first emergence in Spring to dispersal of seeds, is portrayed in a sequence of twelve colour photographs (Pages 49 - 56) following the story.

A *Glossary Of Native, Botanical And Technical Terms* (Pages 57 - 62) completes the book.

Acknowledgements

This story was enhanced by the constructive comments of life-long educator, Anne Smigel, who provided me with the insight of her artistic talents and educational expertise. Rudolf Wagemann, author of many scientific publications, offered editorial suggestions and continuous encouragement throughout the writing of this book. I am grateful to Olenka (Love) Negrych, artist, retired librarian and kindred spirit for her constructive comments and friendship. *Thank you Anne, Rudy and Love, for generously sharing your time and knowledge!*

Photographic consultant and colleague, Peter P. Synychych, facilitated the presentation of photographic images with beneficial suggestions and technical advice.

I thank the many kind individuals and organizations who contributed scientific and traditional ecological knowledge. The guidance of my brother in the Wolf Clan, David Budd (Spirit Name: Pimipahtäw Maskwa, Running Bear) was particularly helpful.

My husband, William Franzin and I have observed and recorded Nature on many memorable field studies. He provided ecological information, editorial assistance and unfaltering support as I pursued my many varied ventures. "Kinanaskomitin nim!"

Mentors Caroline Edwards, Mary Triska, Katherine Wisniewski, Doris Ziehlke and especially Ruth Roper were inspirations in my life. Their collective axiom was, "That load becomes light which is cheerfully borne." (Publius Ovidius Naso, 43BC - 17AD). This became my *modus operandi* in the writing of this book.

Miitik-iikwe
Wolf Clan

A Day On Crocus Hill

With

Sweetgrass

PLATE 1. THE WILD PRAIRIE-CROCUS, *ANEMONE PATENS*.

Centuries ago, when millions of bison roamed the Prairie, a beautiful young maiden named Sweetgrass lived on Mother Earth. With the passage of time, she became an Elder and a powerful Medicine Woman. After many more years among Her People, the mystical Sweetgrass was called to join The Great Spirit. Her Spirit rose from the Earth to walk among the star-flowers in the meadows of the sky.

Sweetgrass still loves and respects Mother Earth. Every year in the Month of Greening, when the days grow longer than the nights, her Spirit returns to the Earthly Domain. On this particular day, a warm ray of spring sunshine carried the venerated Medicine Woman from her celestial home to Mother Earth. The dazzling sunbeam placed her gently on the summit of Crocus Hill, one of the Blue Hills south of Cypress Creek.

Although willowy and beautiful in the dew of life, the grand Medicine Woman appeared as an Elder, bent and bowed with great age. The lines of long years were engraved on her sun-bronzed face. Sweetgrass had sparkling brown eyes that twinkled with love and compassion. In a glance, she could look kindly into your soul. The blossom of an everlasting smile illuminated her high cheekbones and straight nose. She had long silver-white hair plaited neatly into two braids.

Each braid was wound at the end with a strong thread of twisted bison hairs. Three large, white Bald Eagle Honour-feathers were tied into each braid. The old Medicine Woman's hair and feathers sang in the wind and glistened in the sunshine. Sweetgrass wore a choker of finely braided horsehair tied around her neck. This "Story Necklace" was adorned with gifts: animal teeth, quills, claws, bones, pearly shells, red seeds and carved beads of wood and red stone. She favoured the sacred colour red, although all the ornaments were eye-dazzling.

PLATE 2. COMMON BEARBERRY (KINNIKINNICK), *ARCTOSTAPHYLOS UVA-URSI*.

Her smudged ceremonial buckskin dress flowed like soft, silky water over her humble shoulders. The dress was alive with the spirits and prayers of her ancestors. Rows and rows of precious Spirit-seed beads surrounded the oval-shaped neckline of the dress. They formed a broad band of the colours of a rainbow. Colourful glass beads embellished her dress from the neckline down the sleeves to the wide beaded wrist-cuffs. Long buckskin fringes were sewn into the undersides of the sleeves. The fringes continued across both her chest and back below the beaded bodice. When Sweetgrass stretched out her arms, she appeared as a Great Winged Spirit in flight. Beadwork motifs of flowers, animals and the branches of the "Tree of Life" encircled the dress above her knees. The design extended up the sides to her hips, depicting the meeting of Earth and Sky. Three tiers of buckskin fringe decorated the dress below her knees, the lowermost just touching her consecrated moccasins.

PLATE 3. LABRADOR-TEA, *LEDUM GROENLANDICUM.*

Three parfleche pouches were attached to her quilled buckskin bandolier. Her Mystery (Medicine) Bag held Juniper berry-cones, dried Rosehips, Hazelnuts, Acorns, dried seeds of Maize, stalks of Field Mint, dried leaves of Labrador-tea and some fresh pemmican wrapped in parfleche. This pouch also included a Bald Eagle wing feather and her bundle of Four Sacred Smudging Medicines.

Plate 4. Pitcherplant, *Sarracenia purpurea* (Inset: leaf cup).

There were sprigs of Eastern White Cedar and Prairie Sage, Kinnikinnick leaves rolled in red, frost-nipped Silver Maple leaves and a knotted braid of Sweet Grass. It was from the fragrance of this "Holy Grass" that she proudly carried her Spirit Name, Sweetgrass! A smaller, rectangular "Strike-a-light" Bag contained a heart-shaped piece of red flint, a piece of iron, tinder of fine grasses and White Birch punk. A long, narrow Awl Bag, decorated with porcupine quills, contained articles for sewing: a sharp bone needle, elk sinew, threads of softened cedar root and a handful of prickly porcupine quills wrapped in Prairie Bison pericardium. She also carried a green Pitcherplant cup from Berry Creek. It was tied to the outside of the large pouch with twisted strands of horsehair, a symbol of long life.

Sweetgrass wore sacred moccasins possessed of celestial magic. They empowered her to float effortlessly, as freely and lightly as a little downy feather. The Four Wind-Spirits had given her the gift of these soft, smoke-tanned moose-hide moccasins. Each of the Spirits had blessed the shoes. The South-Spirit blew softness and warmth over them. The West-Spirit cast upon them, gentle healing raindrops. The East-Spirit bestowed brightness of peace, while the North-Spirit touched the moccasins with coolness for strength. The beaded vamps, sides and soles of her moccasins were decorated with hearts, star-flowers and leaves. They flashed with the crystal-white of snow, the bright-blue of a clear summer sky, the verdant-green of a tall White Cedar tree, the golden-brown of Mother Earth and the red of the path to the sunset. "The colours of these earthly jewels seem to convey my very thoughts and visions," Sweetgrass mused, as she stood gazing upon her moccasins. The old Medicine Woman shuffled to and fro, embracing her hand-worn Diamond Willow walking stick from Cranberry Carrying Place.

From Crocus Hill, Sweetgrass watched the roaring campfire of the Sun as it burned through the horizon. It blazed forth over the rolling prairie, blushing the surrounding hills like a potter splashing colourful pigments on over-turned clay pots. The black lines of the trees along the meadow edges turned brown and fawn coloured. Gradually, the dark blue-greys of the hills and meadows changed to different shades of golden-brown. Grandfather Sun burst free from the meeting of Earth and Sky in an explosion of light. The new day began with his glorious "Good Morning! It is good to see you all and a special hello to you,

Sweetgrass! I am sure you will enjoy a great day of celebration on Crocus Hill."

Cold-maker and Storm-maker had made Winter on Earth long and cold. Now, almost all the snow was melted except for a few snowbanks on the northern hillsides. Sweetgrass had prayed to the Spirit of the South to blow warm winds over the hills, valleys and lakes. She could feel the heartbeat of Mother Earth and the awakening of new life on Crocus Hill. The streams were trickling again and the first birds of the season were returning from their winter stay in the South.

PLATE 5. WILD PRAIRIE-CROCUS CLUSTER.

"Welcome to you, Sweetgrass," the budding and flowering Prairie-Crocuses around her shouted. "Thank you so much for coming. You are a special guest on our Sacred Prairie Hill. Today, we want to show you many beautiful things. Please sit with us among the golden-brown and green grasses. Let us warm ourselves in the heat of the brilliant Sun." Then the voices of the Wild Prairie-Crocuses, the first flowers heralding Spring, greeted her with the *Song Of The Wild Prairie-Crocus*. The melodious voice of Little Ears, the smallest crocus, rose enthusiastically above the choir.

PLATE 6. CROCUS CUP.

Song Of The Wild Prairie-Crocus

We festive flowers are just for you,
With little coats in shades of blue,
Still dressed in gold and furry paws,
Piercing through the grassy straws.

A crocus flower just for you,
To fill your heart with sunshine through.

The warm Sun has given us strength,
To escape Winter's cold and length.
We give the Spring a sign to start,
Happy to open our golden hearts.

A crocus flower just for you,
To fill your heart with sunshine through.

Chanson Du Crocus Des Prairies

Nous les fleurs de fête sont a toi,
En petites capes de marin bleu,
Nos mains encore velues et jaunes,
En sortant par des herbes sèches.

Une fleur de crocus juste pour toi,
Pour remplir ton coeur de lumière.

Le soleil chaud nous donne la force,
Pour vaincre la longueur d'hiver.
Nous donnons un signe au printemps,
Heureux d'ouvrir nos coeurs dorés.

Une fleur de crocus juste pour toi,
Pour remplir ton coeur de lumière.

PLATE 7. LUMINOUS BUDDING CROCUSES.

Faint little voices called out from the soft, fuzzy buds close to Mother Earth. "Sweetgrass, spend the day with us and our neighbours of the Blue Hills. You will have lots of fun. We admire your warm and beautiful regalia." "Thank you," said Sweetgrass in a measured voice. "You are most thoughtful." The spirits of the Wild Prairie-Crocuses were sacred to her heart. Sweetgrass always learned so much from all the plants and animals of the Earth. She felt privileged to share her precious time with them. Her visit provided an opportunity to exchange knowledge and wisdom with the many living creatures on Crocus Hill.

Just then, Yellow Feathers, the Western Meadowlark, all puffed up in his yellow-breasted coat with a big black V-shape on the front, announced his cheery presence. "I was here-a-year-ago, it's good-to-be-back!" he said. "It is good to see you again and I like your flashy jacket," replied Sweetgrass. She marveled at his colourful plumage and personality. The Ancient Ones had taught her that the birds had received their colours from the sky and the leaves of the trees.

As the Sun rose higher in the eastern sky, life on the hill around her became more animated. The Red Ants quickened their trips with food and building materials. Each ant hurried back and forth to its own family castle. "Look! See how strong we are and what big loads we can carry on our six little legs!" they cried out as they passed the crocuses. "Wow," answered each crocus flower with a cheery smile.

A brown, orange and white butterfly fluttered above the pale, smoky-blue and white crocus patches. It looked like a wind-blown leaf dancing across the tips of the wild prairie grasses. Sometimes, it perched on a crocus flower, spreading out its wings, to warm itself. As if envious, the other neighbouring crocus clusters called out, "Come and rest here!"

Sweetgrass heard a honking sound coming from the southern sky. A large flock of blue and white Snow Geese were flying north in a V-formation. The leader, Kanguq, made a special high-pitched honk. "Ouck, ouck, ouck, hello Sweetgrass, how good it is to see you again! You have such a nice smile, just like each crocus flower on beautiful Crocus Hill!" "Thank you!" replied Sweetgrass. "Have a good trip to your summer home on the Hudson Bay coast near Churchill. Say hello to Nanuq, the Ice Bear and all my friends who live in the True North."

PLATE 8. BEES FORAGE FOR SWEET CROCUS NECTAR AND POLLEN IN EARLY SPRING.

A soft buzzing sound rose from around Sweetgrass's feet. "Another first for this year!" she exclaimed as the honey bees around her gathered sweet nectar from the flowers. Half a dozen golden-brown and black hairy worker-bees buzzed around in one crocus patch. Each of them would circle the centre of a crocus flower before dipping its head deep inside. Sweetgrass watched more closely as one bee combed and gathered all the sticky pollen with her hairy back legs. After a while, her bristle-brush legs were covered with pollen and her two gold-dusted pollen baskets were full. Alas, she had become so heavy that when she tried to fly, she promptly fell down with a KERPLUNK, right on Sweetgrass. When she had recovered her footing she said, "How pretty you are. I heard your noble name carried on the sweet-smelling spring breeze. Do you know that we dance at our nest to show our sisters where to find the fresh spring flowers? Then, they too can gather nectar to make more honey." "Yes," answered Sweetgrass, "and I know that each flower makes a special flavour of honey which always tastes delightful. Thank you for making it. How far is your home from here?" "It is only a short flight northwest of here," replied Buzzy Wings, the busy buzzy bee. "You can see the hill from here. That is why there are so many of us here this morning." "Isn't that too far for you to fly back and forth?" asked Sweetgrass. "Oh, no, not usually," said Buzzy Wings, "but sometimes it is too hot, cold, rainy or windy for us to fly. Then we stay in our Bee Queendom to build more six-sided cells in our waxy combs. Our warm home is inside a hollow high up in an old Bur Oak tree. Would you come to visit us?" "It would be my pleasure," answered Sweetgrass, "I will come by later this afternoon." "Great, by then I will be back with my second collection of Wild Prairie-Crocus nectar," replied Buzzy Wings.

PLATE 9. OPEN CROCUSES REFLECT THE RADIANCE OF THE WARM SPRING SUN.

Sweetgrass turned to watch all the activities in the meadow below Crocus Hill. "Quack, quack, quack," quacked several Mallards that were flying by the hill. They flew west from the marsh to the lake below. She watched a drake and a duck drive the new intruders from the territory in which they had chosen to make their nest. Then Sweetgrass's attention was drawn to an American Kestrel, a small member of the Falcon family. The blue and russet plumed bird was hovering near a grove of tangled Manitoba Maple trees close to the lake. "Klee, klee, klee," cried Arrow, the Kestrel. Suddenly, he dove straight down toward the ground and disappeared into the tall grass. A moment later he reappeared empty-clawed, having missed a fat, furry Deer Mouse. It had escaped into the long prairie grasses. Arrow muttered, "I am a great hunter, I will catch you later! Soon, I will be feasting on small birds, dragonflies, grasshoppers and crickets."

By mid-day all the plants and animals were revelling in the warm Sun. A Red-tailed Hawk was gliding in circles high in the sky, watching everything with his keen, binocular vision, thinking of his next meal. "Skreee, skreee," screeched Flying Cloud, the skilled hunter, as he wheeled round and round, examining the hill for mice and squirrels.

"Caw! Caw! Caw! Caw!" A brash, black American Crow blared loudly. It joined a group of other Crows in the Bur Oak tree bluff on the north side of Crocus Hill. It was a Crow hullabaloo with everyone sharing the latest happenings. "Belabonk, belabonk, belabonk, chay, chay," the sky-blue Blue Jays scolded the Crows. They felt that their friends, the Crows, should have asked for permission before landing on the hill.

Then a high-pitched, plaintive call, "Kill-deer, kill-deer, kill-deer," came up from the marsh. Two Rings, the Killdeer, announced his return from the South to his favourite marsh.

High up, two large black birds came gliding gracefully and silently over Crocus Hill. They looked as large as Eagles to Sweetgrass but by their bald, red heads and their long, fringed, up-arching wings she knew they were soaring Turkey Vultures. The birds sailed easily back and forth across the wind. The carrion-feeders peered this way and that for the bodies of animals that had perished during the Winter. Sweetgrass knew that these "Peace Eagles" were scavengers, playing a part in the cycle of nutrients and energy on Earth.

When the Sun was at the highest point in the sky, Sweetgrass decided it was time for tea. Taking her Pitcherplant cup, she collected a little bead of lemon-coloured dew from each of the Prairie Buttercups nearby. When it was full, the old Medicine Woman placed a few leathery, oval green leaves of Labrador-tea in the cup. Sweetgrass placed the cup of tea on a dark-coloured rock among the

PLATE 10. PRAIRIE BUTTERCUP, *RANUNCULUS RHOMBOIDEUS*.

buttercups to steep in the warmth of the bright Sun. She, like the Ancient Ones, believed that a drink from the Pitcherplant cup bestowed healing and long life.

The old Medicine Woman took some blushed-blue Juniper berry-cones from her Mystery Bag. She placed them in a "Circle of Life" around a knee-high granite boulder in celebration of The Great Spirit and quietly sat down on the ancient stone. It felt good to be sitting on the warm, smooth rock in the middle of the wild prairie flowers on the hill. The warm Sun made Sweetgrass drowsy as she waited for her tea to steep. Nearby, early-blooming Three-flowered Avens swayed gently in the warm spring breeze. Soon, Sweetgrass nodded off into a deep sleep. Her mind, body and spirit became one.

She dreamt about the large rock, which was covered with white, pink, green and orange lichens. Bits of clear quartz and other minerals in the rock sparkled white, pink, red and black in the Sun. They reminded her of the planets and stars where she lived. In her dream, Sweetgrass recalled that such "Grandfather Rocks", born eons before time had spread its wings to the far reaches of the Universe, were part of her world too. When the grand Medicine Woman awoke,

PLATE 11. THREE-FLOWERED AVENS, *GEUM TRIFLORUM* (INSET: SEED STAGE).

she examined her sitting-stone more closely. She realized by its composition that it had travelled to this hill from the far North, moved by glaciers thousands of years ago.

Sweetgrass became aware of what looked like a brown stick standing up in the grass. As if by magic, it fell down and began to run. "Sik-sik, sik-sik," repeated the Thirteen-lined Ground Squirrel. He had come out of one of the many entrance holes to his underground home. Sik-sik's den was his protection from the soaring hawks and other predators. He never ventured far from the safety of its openings. Three times Sik-sik approached Sweetgrass but each time he quickly retreated to his burrow. Sweetgrass sat very still. After a while, Sik-sik came quite close and proceeded to inspect her. Sweetgrass realized that she was sitting right next to one of the tunnels. "I'm sorry I disturbed you," she said. Sik-sik did not reply but feeling comforted, he sat down and proudly stretched out his long body to show off his thirteen stripes. There was no more fear.

Sweetgrass picked up her cup and sipped some tea. Her Pitcherplant cup of spring dew tea was a drink of pure goodness. To have tea honoured The Creator. She unwrapped some pemmican, the finest source of nourishment the Earth had to offer. The dried meat and fat held the majestic Spirit of the Prairie Bison. The seeds, berries and nuts held the knowledge of all the plants around her. Through it, she shared in the spirit and life of many living things. After finishing her tea and pemmican, she gave thanks to The Great Spirit, the provider of all life. The Medicine Woman pressed her left foot and then her left hand into the soft golden-brown and green grasses as token kisses to Mother Earth.

PLATE 12. PURPLE CROCUS FLOWER GOBLET.

Sweetgrass rose slowly and bent down to study the magnificence of Nature in the crocus bunch next to her. Each velvety flower displayed extraordinary harmony of form and colour. The individual blossoms were about as wide as the length of her little finger. She saw that the flowers had six to eight sepals forming circular flower-goblets. The leafless erect stem had six frosted-green, crowfoot-shaped leaves at its base. The pale, smoky-blue flowers varied from pastel shades of blue-violet on the inside to just a hint of violet on the outside.

PLATE 13. THE RARE WHITE COLOUR VARIATION OF THE WILD PRAIRIE-CROCUS.

PLATE 14. A CLUSTER OF RARE WHITE WILD PRAIRIE-CROCUSES.

Close by, crocus clusters bloomed in pale blue, purple and even white. All around her on the Blue Hills, the blankets of flowers swayed with the rhythmic breathing of the wind, creating waves of colours. It was as if animal-spirits were running wildly across the rolling hills. The softened porcupine quills that decorated her Awl Bag were dyed with the extracts of the golden centres and blue sepals of crocuses. Sweetgrass had travelled the world and knew other names and uses for the Wild Prairie-Crocus in the many lands where it grows.

The golden heart of a nearby tiny crocus reflected a ray of sunshine into the eyes of Sweetgrass, rousing her from her reverie. "Look at the beautiful warm, woolly cape that I'm wearing," Little Ears, the crocus flower, said to Sweetgrass. "I close my sepal cape to keep my golden heart warm and to protect me during cold, windy days and frosty nights. Often, we have to face many days of harsh snowstorms and freezing temperatures. Still, we survive." "I know," replied Sweetgrass, "you do have a colourful, downy coat. It must even protect you from drying out on hot, dry days. All of your relations are rising from Mother Earth and they are getting dressed too. Together, you look like a flock of little furry goslings of many colours: brown, yellow, green and pink. You are all wonderfully dressed!" "Thank you," smiled Little Ears. "We are so happy to present to you our fuzzy spring garments." "Soon," said Sweetgrass, "your blossoms will follow Grandfather Sun across the sky every day to keep your hearts warm. Your golden hearts always glow with the goodness of sunshine, just as all our hearts should. I know that your thick, woody taproots go deep into the hill to drink from the water of the snowmelt. You sense the awakening of all the natural things in Spring before all the other flowers. When you poke your little heads out of Mother Earth, I know Spring has begun. Later, you will release fine grey feather-dusters that carry your seeds on the Four Winds. Together, we grow deep roots of friendship that enrich our lives. Thank you so much for showing me your unique prairie clothes. I truly enjoyed sharing this time with you. Now, I must pay a visit to the honey bees at Bee Queendom. I'll be back by sunset when I will see you again."

PLATE 15. SEED STAGE OF THE WILD PRAIRIE-CROCUS.

Sweetgrass set off along an animal trail that she knew would lead to Bee Queendom. It was much farther by trail than Buzzy Wing's short flight across the hills. Walking down the hill and into the meadow, she heard Yellow Feathers, the Western Meadowlark, call out in his tinkling voice, "Hello again, Sweetgrass, I think I know where I'm going to build my nest this year." Sweetgrass already knew how he would build his "secret" grass nest. His little grass hut would be difficult to find because the entrance would be a long tunnel hidden in the grass. "I hope you have a pleasant Summer," wished Sweetgrass.

She continued along the winding path by the marsh, admiring the many new spring arrivals. The waxy, yellow Marsh-marigolds and the Yellow Lady's-slippers along the marsh-edge were sprouting but in the water, the Yellow Pond-lilies still were below the surface. Sweetgrass noticed patches of Field Mint and Prairie Sage among the grasses. She stepped off the path to gather a few fresh sprigs to replenish her supply of medicines. The Medicine Woman tied each bunch of herbs into a little bundle with a thread of dry grass and placed them into her Mystery Bag. Sweetgrass paused to inhale the lingering aroma on her fingertips.

PLATE 16. UPPER LEFT: MARSH-MARIGOLD, *CALTHA PALUSTRIS*; LOWER LEFT: PRAIRIE SAGE, *ARTEMISIA LUDOVICIANA*; RIGHT: FIELD MINT, *MENTHA ARVENSIS*.

PLATE 17. YELLOW LADY'S-SLIPPER, *CYPRIPEDIUM CALCEOLUS*.

The old Medicine Woman caught the scent of her namesake, Sweet Grass, rising from around her feet. A few tiny, pointed leaves of the grass curled out from under her moccasins. Slowly, she bent down and pinched a blade of the Sacred Medicine between her fingers to release the fragrance. Sweetgrass said to herself, "Soon, The Great Spirit will bring the season of long days of brightness and growth over Mother Earth. Then the animals will enjoy the long, narrow leaves of the tall, fresh-scented Sweet Grass." Returning to the path, Sweetgrass saw little blushing buds of rosy-pink Bog Laurels peeking out from under a Pussy Willow bush. Next to them, she spied the fleshy, green leaves of Wintergreen. She simply could not resist tasting a few of the remaining reddish-brown berries of last year. Their aroma and taste was overpowering and refreshing.

PLATE 18. LEFT: FLORETS OF SWEET GRASS, *HIEROCHLOË ODORATA*; RIGHT: PINK WINTERGREEN, *PYROLA ASARIFOLIA*.

PLATE 19. PRINCE'S-PINE (WINTERGREEN), *CHIMAPHILA UMBELLATA*.

PLATE 20. UPPER LEFT: WESTERN CANADA VIOLET, *VIOLA RUGULOSA*; UPPER RIGHT: COMMON BLUE-EYED GRASS, *SISYRINCHIUM MONTANUM*; BOTTOM: ARUM-LEAVED ARROWHEAD, *SAGITTARIA CUNEATA*.

The old Medicine Woman continued walking slowly, step by step, then stood and leaned on her Diamond Willow stick, to rest for a while. The lush green moss felt like cool soft feathers beneath her feet. Nearby, the sweet white buds of Western Canada Violets, veined with pink and purple, rested on a bed of green

PLATE 21. BLUE FLAG, *IRIS VERSICOLOR*.

heart-shaped leaves. Sweetgrass saw tiny green sprouts of Arum-leaved Arrowheads just below the surface of the water in the marsh. Later in the season, their flowers of three pure white petals and yellow centres would bask in the Sun. Even the tall green shafts of the Cattails had made a start. The exquisite Common Blue-eyed Grass and the tall Blue Flags were just beginning to sprout. Sweetgrass was enchanted by the life and beauty brought forth by Spring.

She began to climb up the hill toward Bee Queendom and entered a large grove of tall Trembling Aspen. A small brook bubbled and burbled its way down the hill, through the trees, toward the lake. Looking back to where the little stream

PLATE 22. YELLOW POND-LILY, *NUPHAR VARIEGATUM*.

entered the lake, she noticed a small herd of Prairie Bison. Newly born calves were running friskily among the cows and bulls. They were grazing on early grasses along the lakeshore. Sweetgrass carefully made her way along the side of the brook, pausing occasionally to listen to her friends, the Laughing Waters. She came upon a thicket of Diamond Willows. They rattled in the breeze and said, "We are proud that one of our strong saplings helps you on your way."

All at once, a large, stately animal appeared in front of her. It was Leaping Willow, the rare White-tailed Deer, grunting and snorting. He was coming down the same trail from the opposite direction. Leaping Willow recognized the old Medicine Woman immediately and said in his deep husky voice, "Well, hello, sweetest of all the grasses! I was wondering when I would meet you this Spring." Leaping Willow also was a very wise Elder. Recently, he had shed his grand antlers, leaving him bare-headed and cool for the Spring. Sweetgrass knew that the many points of his antlers reflected his years of experience of living in the bush. He was shedding his heavy winter coat too, anticipating the warm weather ahead. "It is good to see you again," answered Sweetgrass warmly, "and how is your doe?" "Just fine," replied Leaping Willow. "In two moons, she will give birth to one or two beautiful, light brown spotted fawns. We hope to have a doe and a buck. The new life will make us happy and proud. My family will stay deep in the woods up the hill. Now that it is getting warmer, the shade and safety of the forest will be a comfort to us. I will keep a close watch over them." "I am sure

PLATE 23. BEAKED HAZELNUT, *CORYLUS CORNUTA*; LEFT: FLOWER; RIGHT: TWINNED NUT.

you will be a devoted father. Your doe and expected little ones are most fortunate," said Sweetgrass. The old Medicine Woman resumed her journey along the path towards Bee Queendom.

The trail offered more interesting sights. The tiny, frilly crimson flowers of the Hazelnut bushes were beginning to show. "You are so petite, intricate and beautiful. To see you, one must stop and look," said Sweetgrass quietly. "Thank you!" a little voice piped back. "We Hazelnuts appreciate that you notice us."

PLATE 24. GREAT HORNED OWL, *BUBO VIRGINIANUS*; STORY NAME: TIGER HILLS OWL.

A low, sonorous voice then came from a large high branch of an old White Spruce tree. "Who? Who-oo? Who? Who are you? Is it you, Sweetgrass?" hooted Tiger Hills Owl, a grizzly, greyish-brown Great Horned Owl. He was as tall as a large goose and had two big feathery ears, big round yellow eyes and a large sharply-hooked beak. The Owl held onto the branch with large black claws that protruded from his feathered feet.

Sweetgrass remembered the story of the first dance and how Owl's beak became bent. Long ago, in the first Pow-wow, Owl was asleep and awoke to see Wasikejak, the Dancing Spirit, trying to wring the necks of the geese. The Spirit told Owl to close his eyes and dance. Then he punched Owl in the beak, forever changing its shape.

"Yes, it is I," answered Sweetgrass from down below. "I was hoping you would be here, it is always nice to meet a knowledgeable Elder." "You flatter me," said Tiger Hills Owl smiling. "You can observe so much from your home in the sky. You are the real wise one! Thank you for coming again this year to marvel at all the living things. You give all of us the courage and hope to fulfill our destinies!" "Indeed," said Sweetgrass. "In order to notice goodness and beauty, one must learn to stop, look, listen and contemplate. My, aren't we fortunate that we learned wisdom and respect from our Elders?" concluded Sweetgrass. Tiger Hills Owl closed his enormous saucer-shaped eyes and bowed down in humble approval. Sweetgrass asked, "Have you had your nap this afternoon? I recall that you do take at least twenty minutes of shut-eye after EVERY meal except breakfast." "No, no-oo, no, no, I was just about to take a little rest right now," responded the gruff old Owl as his head drooped forward on his chest.

PLATE 25. SASKATOON, *AMELANCHIER ALNIFOLIA*; LEFT: FLOWER; RIGHT: BERRY.

PLATE 26. WESTERN RED LILY, *LILIUM PHILADELPHICUM*.

Sweetgrass continued on the trail up the hill, passing by some thick Saskatoon bushes. Closing her eyes she prayed, "Let your blossoms be spared heavy rains, strong winds, killing frosts and the scorching Sun. May you bear many tasty berries for all to eat." She approached the top of the hill where the bush gradually opened to reveal a large grassy area.

An old, gnarly, greyish-brown Bur Oak tree stood in full sun near the northern edge of the hilltop meadow. A hollow, high up in the trunk of the branching

PLATE 27. LONG-HEADED CONEFLOWER, *RATIBIDA COLUMNIFERA*.

tree, was the heart of Bee Queendom. The southerly spring breeze floated the scent of flowers right up to the hollow. Sweetgrass had arrived just in time to see Buzzy Wings arriving with another load of crocus nectar and glowing pollen.

"Welcome!" cried Buzzy Wings. "Thank you," replied Sweetgrass. "There are so many of you here!" Indeed, there were swarms of busy bees. On this warm day, the place was humming with activity. Buzzy Wings carried her load into the hollow tree nest, staying long enough to convert it into honey and place it into

PLATE 28. WESTERN WILD BERGAMOT, *MONARDA FISTULOSA*.

an ivory-coloured comb of beeswax. Sweetgrass could only imagine how hard and long the bees had worked to make their honey. Buzzy Wings came back out to visit with Sweetgrass.

"How did you bees find Crocus Hill?" Sweetgrass asked. Buzzy Wings began speaking slowly at first but then "Bzzzz, bzzzz, bzzzz," faster and faster she chatted with Sweetgrass. "Oh, worker-bees go out every day to forage for nectar and pollen. The tiny, delicate crocuses are the first flowers to appear in Spring. Our swarm follows the fragrant scent that the flowers send on the breeze. We flit and fly about having flower-fun and sip nectar with our long tongues. Our

PLATE 29. FLODMAN'S THISTLE, *CIRSIUM FLODMANII.*

compass, Grandfather Sun, warms us up with his rays in the morning. We hunt for patches of nectar-rich flowers. When one of us finds a productive patch, she returns to the Queen's Court to dance in front of all the other worker-bees. For direction, North to South, busy as a bee she wiggles. For distance, East to West, buzzing she waggles." Buzzy Wings buzzed her wings wildly as she talked.

"That's wonderful!" exclaimed Sweetgrass but before she could say more, Buzzy Wings interrupted her. "Yes, we sing, buzzing all day, while zipping from flower to flower. We remember the colour, shape and position of flowers to direct the others. We bees see four colours: yellow, orange and green appear as one,

PLATE 30. UPPER LEFT: MARSH-MARIGOLD, *CALTHA PALUSTRIS*; UPPER RIGHT: SHINING ARNICA, *ARNICA FULGENS*; LOWER LEFT: GREAT-FLOWERED GAILLARDIA, *GAILLARDIA ARISTATA*; LOWER RIGHT: BLACK-EYED SUSAN, *RUDBECKIA HIRTA*.

blue-green is the second, blue-violet is the third and unlike you, we also see ultraviolet. All the flowers throughout the seasons are precious to us. We particularly favour yellow, blue and violet blossoms." "What are some of those flowers?" asked Sweetgrass. "First," replied Buzzy Wings, "in the Month of Greening, we find Prairie-Crocuses, Prairie Buttercups, Three-flowered Avens, Hazelnuts and Marsh-marigolds. Later in the Spring, we drink from the flowers of

PLATE 31. SCARLET PAINTBRUSH, *CASTILLEJA COCCINEA*.

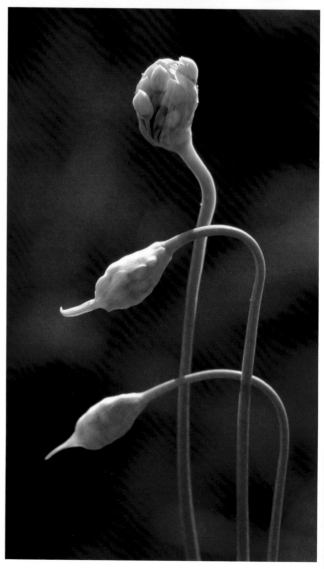

PLATE 32. TOP: WILD CUCUMBER, *ECHINOCYSTIS LOBATA*; LEFT: COMMON HOP, *HUMULUS LUPULUS*; RIGHT: BUDS OF PRAIRIE ONION, *ALLIUM STELLATUM*.

PLATE 33. MEADOW BLAZINGSTAR, *LIATRIS LIGULISTYLIS*; LEFT: FLOWER; RIGHT: SEED STAGE.

the fruiting shrubs and trees like Saskatoon, American Plum, Black-fruited Choke Cherry and Pin Cherry. We even visit Manitoba Maple, Bur Oak, Trembling Aspen and Pussy Willow trees to collect their especially flavourful nectars."

Buzzy Wings became so excited, there was no interrupting her. "We can hardly wait to taste sweet-scented, pink Wild Prairie Roses and the white flowers of Wild Cucumber. Beautiful Yellow and Scarlet Paintbrushes blush when we stroke their bracts. The fiery bursts of the black-dotted Western Red Lilies are very enticing to us. Our bristle-brush back legs touch the purple and pink points of Meadow Blazingstar, Western Wild Bergamot, Flodman's Thistle, Stinging Nettle and Prairie Onion. We buzz around and land on the papery cone-shaped blooms of Common Hop and the hard, spiny heads of Purple and Long-headed Coneflowers. The colourful, ambrosial flowers tickle us all over."

PLATE 34. TOP: PRAIRIE ONION, *ALLIUM STELLATUM*; BOTTOM: YARROW, *ACHILLEA MILLEFOLIUM*.

PLATE 35. PURPLE CONEFLOWER, *ECHINACEA ANGUSTIFOLIA*.

"Buzzy Wings, what are the last blooms of the season?" asked Sweetgrass. The bee stopped to think. Then she broke into a big, wide, watermelon-grin and rolled her round, faceted, googly eyes. "Summer usually ends with a blaze of glorious gold: Great-flowered Gaillardia, Black-eyed Susans, Prairie Sunflowers, Shining Arnica and Velvety Goldenrods. We love to dive into the white, woolly clouds of Yarrow and there is nothing like a rest on the soft, white rays of Wild Chamomile. We visit the many star-shaped Asters of white, blue and purple. There are so many other kinds of flowers that I have not mentioned. I love each one of them! I'll write their names in beeswax on a piece of White Birch bark. It will come floating down the little spring brook to you. Then you will know all the miraculous wildflowers that we will visit in the coming blossom time."

"Marvelous!" exclaimed Sweetgrass. "It is easy to understand why your honey is so flavourful and sweet." Buzzy Wings continued, "We help the plants to make their seeds by carrying pollen from flower to flower. It is a fair exchange for all the nectar they give us." "Yes, it is amazing how Mother Earth helps us all to help one another," said Sweetgrass. Buzzy Wings then said, "I do hope you will enjoy some of our wonderful Crocus Honey. I will ask our Queen Bee to let you sample some of it." "That would be delightful," replied Sweetgrass. Her eyes followed Buzzy Wings as she flew up to the hollow in the tree. A moment later, a powerful, deep buzzing sound was heard. "BZZZZZ! BZZZZZZ! BZZZZZZ!" Several worker-bees appeared at the entrance of the nest. The Royal Guards lined up for inspection by Rose Heart, "The Queen Of The Bees".

PLATE 36. WILD PRAIRIE ROSE, *ROSA* SPECIES (INSET: ROSEHIPS; SEED STAGE).

"Your Majesty," announced Buzzy Wings, "this is Sweetgrass from the star-filled sky!" "How do you do, venerable Sweetgrass?" said the large, portly Queen Bee. "We are honoured by your presence at our Royal Court." "Likewise, I am enchanted to be in the company of your Royal Highness," said Sweetgrass, as she exchanged glances of recognition with Royal Rose Heart. "It is always extraordinary to see what work you and your subjects do!"

Queen Rose Heart made a motion and vibrated her four iridescent wings with royal splendour. She performed an Imperial Bee Dance with deliberate dignity. Then the Queen Bee commanded a member of her Royal Guards to bring a droplet of Crocus Honey for Sweetgrass. "Let her taste of the sweet power of the first flowers of Spring," said Her Majesty. The attendant worker-bee went into the hive and returned with a tiny beeswax jug filled with Crocus Honey. She flew down and presented the gift onto the Medicine Woman's open palm. Sweetgrass raised the jug to her mouth and squeezed out a golden drop of honey onto her tongue. All the bees, with their big faceted eyes, watched with approval.

"Oh, this is truly delicious, there is absolutely no other taste like it! It gives me a feeling of warmth and energy," she exclaimed. "I can taste every crocus flower in it. Thank you for being so very kind!" "You are most welcome, my dear, please grace us with your presence again soon," said the Queen Bee. The Royal Guards saluted as Queen Rose Heart turned to withdraw into her chambers. The Queen Bee nodded to acknowledge each of the guards as she passed. The subjects followed her into the nest. The Queen then returned to laying eggs and supervising the feeding of larvae, making of bee bread and chinking of cells.

Buzzy Wings and Sweetgrass were alone again. Buzzy Wings flew around and brushed her hairy body on Sweetgrass's nose. It tickled her and almost made her sneeze. "Buzzy, you have shown me today your secret art of making honey," Sweetgrass whispered. "Thank you so much for sharing your time and helping me to appreciate all that you do." "You are most welcome. Now, I really must resume collecting nectar and pollen to feed our newly-hatched larvae. I can gather one more load of crocus nectar today," said Buzzy Wings, as she buzzed off toward Crocus Hill. Sweetgrass turned slowly, so as not to startle the bees and proceeded back down the hill.

PLATE 37. A SPIDER AND A BEE REST BRIEFLY ON A PRAIRIE-CROCUS FLOWER TO ABSORB WARMTH FROM THE SUN ON A CHILLY MORNING.

When she came to the brook, she noticed little silvery fishes swimming around in the fast-moving water. They were Creek Chubs, Fathead Minnows and Brook Sticklebacks migrating up the stream to feed and spawn. Northern Crayfish were crawling among the cobblestones and gravel looking for food.

Then she noticed a sleek, shiny, brown furry animal about the size of her forearm crouched on the overhanging bank. It was Slick Water, the Mink. He was staring intently at the fish. "Those little fishes and crayfish would make a tasty dinner," he said in a rough, throaty voice. "You had better let them spawn first or there won't be any fish for you to eat next year," replied Sweetgrass.

She continued on her way along the edge of the marsh toward Crocus Hill. A chorus of Red-winged Blackbirds trilled "Chit-chit-chirree" from their perches in the Trembling Aspen trees bordering the marsh. Their songs expressed the joy they felt upon returning to the wetland of their birth. Here they would raise new families. During the breaks in the chorus, a solo male Song Sparrow interjected his distinctive cheery song, "Cheer, cheer, cheer, it's a joy, Spring is here!"

As Sweetgrass passed by an open-water section of the marsh, she was greeted by a frog symphony. Four distinct parts were being sung. Sometimes only a solo was heard, while at other times the voices swelled into a harmonious chorus. A Spring Peeper provided a soprano solo part by his repeated peeps, "Pee-eep, pee-eep." The brown Wood Frog joined in as the alto with an excited guttural clucking, "Gal-uk, gal-uk-gal-uk-gal-uk." A group of Boreal Chorus Frogs, with their high-pitched calls, "Krreak, krreak, krreak" made up the soprano choir of the frog ensemble. A lonely Northern Leopard Frog added his baritone stutter, going high to low and fast to slow, "Uh-uh-uh-uh-uh-uh." Even though Sweetgrass's steps were very quiet, the chorus stopped abruptly! The frog choir had seen movement. Sweetgrass stood motionless. Soon the whole chorus began again, even louder than before. The amphibians accepted her attention and appreciation with deep gratitude. The warmth of Sweetgrass's presence made them sing even faster.

Back at the lower meadow, Yellow Feathers, the Western Meadowlark and Two Rings, the Killdeer, were busily arranging their nesting sites. More ducks had arrived at the lake. Northern Pintail and Blue-winged Teal drakes impressed their mates with all sorts of aquatic acrobatics. This display of energy pleased Sweetgrass. It reassured her that the power of life in Nature was as it should be.

At the foot of Crocus Hill, she came upon a copse of Round-leaved Hawthorn. The shrub's reddish-brown, needle-like thorns were as long as her fingers but unlike her fingers, they were thin, straight and very sharp. "No one can go in there," murmured Sweetgrass to herself. "On the contrary, we're safe in here!" a snappy voice chided from a branch overhead. Running Fire, the Red Squirrel, flicked his rusty-red tail and pointed down to a brownish-grey and white Eastern Cottontail crouched beneath the spiny bushes. "Running Fire is right," agreed Moon Dancer, the timid little rabbit. "Only we know the entrances to the Hawthorn thicket. Our enemies the Hawks, Red Fox, American Badger, Coyote and Grey Wolf fear to enter here because of the sharp needles of our friends, the Hawthorns." "Just thinking about it makes me cringe!" said Sweetgrass. Running Fire replied, "We are fortunate to have this safe place. Many warblers, sparrows, orioles and other small migratory birds share our shelter." "Good for you!" replied Sweetgrass. "I am always pleased to see how Mother Earth looks after you smaller beings."

PLATE 38. WILD PRAIRIE-CROCUSES BEGIN TO CLOSE WITH THE SETTING OF THE SUN.

Sweetgrass climbed up Crocus Hill again as the glowing Sun was sinking fast in the West. Each crocus flower was furling its sepals to protect its golden heart from the cool of the night.

Little Ears whispered, "Thank you again for coming to visit us. Why don't you watch the sunset from here? This evening, it will be spectacular! Most of my sisters and brothers have gone to sleep. I hope you will stay until dark. Your presence is comforting. You radiate inner beauty, kindness and warmth, Sweetgrass." These words from Little Ears made Sweetgrass feel very loved by all of the residents on the hill. They gave her new strength. She knew that all things have a purpose and that life with inner balance and harmony is more powerful than any frost or cold wind. All day, she had experienced kindness everywhere and beauty in everything. "What a splendid time I had on Crocus Hill!" thought Sweetgrass, contentedly.

The colours of the Sun setting over the Blue Hills changed from golden brown to a deep rusty brown. Shadows lengthened across the meadows. A long, high cloud over the sinking Sun became rosy-red, then mauve. The white planets, Mercury and Venus, appeared and reminded Sweetgrass of other beautiful members of the Solar System.

Slowly and gracefully, Sweetgrass turned to the East and raised her head to The Creator with respect and humility. Her face was illuminated by the magnificent, silvery full Moon rising above the hills. The sky had changed from blue to violet to black. The light of Grandmother Moon and the stars cast faint shadows over the Blue Hills. "Good night, my dear brothers and sisters," said Sweetgrass to all the plants and animals, "may The Great Spirit smile upon you!"

All around her the plants and animals had been busy all day and now most of them rested blissfully. The Doe was lying down among the trees while Leaping Willow stood watch. The Mink, Red Fox, American Badger, Coyote and Grey Wolf had wandered off the hill on their nightly treks into the meadows to check the far corners of their territories. The Red Squirrel, Thirteen-lined Ground Squirrel and Eastern Cottontail were curled up in their nests. The birds quietly huddled together with all their feathers puffed up to keep warm. They sat on perches in trees and nestled into pockets of grass. Down at the lake, the ducks floated and dozed with their heads tucked under their wings, occasionally opening a watchful eye. In the marsh, all the frogs were raising their chorus high. The fish and crayfish were wriggling among the stones in the shallow stream feeding on aquatic insects. The butterfly had folded up its wings and hung upside down from the underside of a twig. The bees had retired earlier in the evening to spend the night in the warmth of their nest high up in the old Bur Oak tree. The ants had descended into the deeper, warmer galleries of their castle to rest until the morning.

Tiger Hills Owl came gliding over Crocus Hill toward Sweetgrass. He observed that everything was serene and still. The wise Elder, drifted silently down through the pale moonlight to Sweetgrass. Softly, he whispered into her ear, "May the Moon and stars guide you on your journey to The Great Spirit." Respectfully, Owl left as quietly as he came. Rising gently upward on his large feathery wings, he vanished into the darkened forest.

PLATE 39. A FEATHERY PRAIRIE-CROCUS SEED.

It was with a happy heart that Sweetgrass looked up into the starry sky. She closed her eyes and folded her arms across her chest. The Medicine Woman invoked the magic of her beaded moccasins and the low, thunderous drum of Mother Earth's heartbeat rumbled across the hill. The star-flowers of her moccasins flashed and danced in a profusion of colours, surrounding Sweetgrass with an aura of light. She floated up lightly into the warm night sky, like a feathery seed of a Wild Prairie-Crocus on a spring breeze. Sweetgrass rose

PLATE 40. *SWEETGRASS*, A DENIZEN OF THE SKY, JOURNEYS AMONG THE CELESTIAL STAR-FLOWERS LIKE THE EPHEMERAL COMET HALE-BOPP, SHOWN HERE.

slowly at first, then ascended faster and faster, until she disappeared among the twinkling stars. Suddenly, an explosion of scintillating sparkles showered down, enveloping Crocus Hill in a shimmering veil of light. An atmosphere of tranquility cloaked the hill, bringing peace to all of its inhabitants. All the plants and animals were snug and cozy in the knowledge that the kind old Medicine Woman would continue to watch over them from above.

The natural cycle of life on Mother Earth continues...

The Life Cycle Of The Wild Prairie-Crocus Flower

Many people associate the arrival of Spring on the Prairies with the emergence of the Wild Prairie-Crocuses on their local "Crocus Hill". The ten to fourteen day *Life Cycle Of The Wild Prairie-Crocus Flower* is shown in the following sequence of twelve botanical photographs.

The flowers emerge from the lingering snow in early Spring. They begin as soft fuzzy buds of golden-brown, green and pink peeking out from among the brown and grey blades of decaying grass (Page 49). The Wild Prairie-Crocuses then develop into silky-haired, iridescent, closed tulip-shapes (Page 50). The blooms open outward as the stems lengthen (Page 51). The flower stage culminates in a beautiful, fully open mauve, or rarely, white, blossom (Pages 52-54). Finally, the bloom transforms into the fruiting stage. The stalks lengthen further and the coloured sepals dry and fall away (the Wild Prairie-Crocus doesn't have petals). A heart-shaped receptacle anchors a greyish-white globular seed head of many fine feathery achenes (Page 55). At the end, the achenes blow off on the warm spring winds (Page 56).

Glossary Of Native, Botanical And Technical Terms

Achene: A dry, hard thin-walled single seed that does not open when ripe.

Acorn: The edible fruit (nut) of a Bur Oak tree that is partially enclosed in a fringed cup.

Ancient Ones: Spirits of ancestors who have passed along their knowledge and wisdom to the present generation through stories and folklore.

Animal-Spirits: First Nations people attribute animal-spirit powers to the Four Wind directions: North (Buffalo), South (Mouse), East (Eagle) and West (Bear). The Spirits may be manifested by the action of the wind blowing through the trees or across a field of grass, giving the appearance of the movements of animals.

Awl: A needle constructed of a hard material such as animal bone, wood, stone or metal for piercing holes in material.

Awl Bag: A hard leather bag for carrying awls.

Bald Eagle Feather: In the story, the Mystical Sweetgrass wears Eagle feathers as an indication of the highest honour bestowed by The Creator. A gift of feathers from the Eagle (its living breath) to another person is to honour love, great friendship, loyalty and bravery.

Bandolier: A strip of material worn over the shoulder and across the chest to support a bag or other article.

Bead: A colourful object such as a piece of glass, shell, stone, metal or wood that has been carved, ground and polished into a round, oblong, oval or animal shape and fitted with a hole for stringing. Padre, Peking, Russian, Watermelon and White-heart are a few of the names of glass "trader beads".

Bee Bread: A mixture of honey and pollen produced and stored by bees for food during cold weather and in the Winter.

Berry Creek: A small creek running into eastern Lake Of The Woods, Ontario, Canada. Sweetgrass enjoys visiting a small waterfall there in Summer.

Blue Hills: Presently known as the Tiger Hills of south-central Manitoba, Canada.

Bracts: A modified leaf structure on a plant that supports a flower.

Buckskin: A tanned deer hide that is scraped clean, stretched, smoked with rotted wood or conifer cones (for colourant), rubbed with brains to soften it and washed with water.

Bundle: A bundle may encompass many things: e.g., medicines, tools, a drum, flute or rattle, skills and knowledge that help one walk the path of life. A human life is a gift from The Creator. Therefore, a person is responsible to care for and share his or her bundle(s) with others.

Castle: In the story, an ant hill constructed of soil and other particles above and below the ground.

Chinking of Cells: Sealing up the cells in a bee comb.

Churchill: Manitoba's only seaport, located on the east side of the mouth of the Churchill River at Hudson Bay, Canada.

Circle of Life: In Aboriginal (First Nations) culture the Circle of Life represents balance and harmony between Man and Nature, birth through death, the seasons of the year, the movements of the stars, winds and water currents.

Cold-maker and Storm-maker: Northerly winds bring cold and storms to instill strength and endurance in all organisms.

Comet Hale-Bopp: This comet was discovered by Alan Hale and Thomas Bopp on July 2, 1995. It appeared to the naked eye in March and April, 1997. This was the largest comet to pass near Earth since 1577. Originally it was calculated to return again in about 4,000 years but due to its close passage by Jupiter, its future orbit changed to return it near Earth in about 2,380 years. To Sweetgrass, the comet was a "celestial star-flower" of the sky.

Copse: A little grove of shrubs or trees with an interior open area.

Cranberry Carrying Place: Named as such in 1791; presently the town of Cranberry Portage, Manitoba, Canada.

Crocus Hill: Any of the many well-drained prairie hills on which Wild Prairie-Crocuses thrive.

Crocus Honey: Honey made by bees only from crocus nectar.

Crowfoot: The shape of the leaf of the Wild Prairie-Crocus resembling the imprint of a crow's footprint.

Cypress Creek: Presently called Cypress River, located in south-central Manitoba, Canada.

Dancing Spirit: A trickster; in Cree, "Wasikejack"*; in Ojibwa, "Nanabouzhou"*. The Dancing Spirit could assume different forms and speak with plants and animals. *Various spellings in the different languages.

Elder: A respected Aboriginal (First Nations) person possessed of great wisdom who shares cultural values, traditions, healing arts, language, history, ceremonies, songs and prayers.

Elk Sinew: Sinews are single long filaments taken from the Achille's tendon of the hind legs of the elk and used as sewing thread.

Googly Eyes: Wobbly big eyes which stare independently from side to side.

"Grandfather Rocks": Rocks are like grandfathers, they are very old and we learn from their long experience.

Grandfather Sun: In this story, the Sun is the provider of all energy and lights the day on Mother Earth like a glowing campfire.

Grandmother Moon: In this story, Mother of the Earth, a Spirit that gives the night light and moves great waters.

Great Spirit: Also known as The Kind One or The Creator, The Great Spirit is not owned by anyone and belongs to all people.

Handprint and Footprint: The pressing of a left hand and a left foot into the ground to make prints is a sign of peace to Mother Earth.

Horsehair: The horse was an important gift from The Creator to people of First Nations. Horsehair is used as thread or braided for sacred, ornamental and functional purposes, e.g., wrapping pipe stems, in headdresses and fans, making necklaces and rope. Long horsehair strands symbolize a long life.

Infusion: Steeping or soaking herbaceous leaves in hot water to make a liquid extract. For example, a blend of Labrador-tea leaves and Eastern White Cedar leaves may be used as a healing medicine.

Kinnikinnick (Bearberry): Dried leaves are used by First Nations as a Sacred Medicine. The leaves typically are stored in baskets or long rectangular parfleche bags. It is used and given in respect; for sharing and blessing of words passed between two people in honesty. The Kinnikinnick is offered in prayer. The smoke of the burning leaves travels as a messenger to communicate with The Great Spirit. Old spelling: K'nick K'neck.

Medicine Woman: Story Name: Sweetgrass, a Mystery Woman and respected Elder. She carries her Medicine Bundle containing the "Four Sacred Medicines": Kinnikinnick, Sweet Grass, Eastern White Cedar and Prairie Sage.

Moccasin: A soft kind of shoe made from a tanned deer, elk or moose hide, often trimmed or lined with fur. There are many styles from low to high, from simple to highly decorative. Modern moccasins may be made of commercially tanned leather and many other different materials. Sweetgrass's moccasins were smudged, i.e., purified and cleansed with Prairie Sage in prayer to The Creator and were "protected".

Month of Greening: The first month of Spring when fresh grasses and herbs sprout up and the trees produce new green leaves.

Mother Earth: Mother Earth, the sustainer of life in Aboriginal (First Nations) culture, represents many aspects of existence in the presence of Grandfather Sun.

Parfleche: Dried, untanned animal hide (skin).

Pemmican: Various mixtures of edible berries: e.g., Blueberry, High Bush-Cranberry, Creeping Juniper, Saskatoon, combined with Acorns, Beaked Hazelnuts and Pin, Choke or Sand cherries, all ground together with dried animal meat, bone marrow and fat.

Porcupine Quills: Porcupine quills are long, sharp hollow shafts of modified hair evolved for the animal's defense against predators. These quills are used for decorative purposes by people of many First Nations. The quills are washed, cleaned and softened in water. The sharp ends of the quills are pierced. Then they may be dyed in different colours with plant and mineral extracts. Flattened quills are sewn onto baskets and clothing like embroidery threads. Specialist quill artisans are called *quillers*.

Pow-wow: Algonkian word (early spelling, Pau-Wau) meaning a "Celebration of Life" where people, led by healers and spiritual leaders, come together to dance and feast.

Prairie Bison Pericardium: The dried skin of the surrounding sac of a bison heart. Sweetgrass wrapped sharp items in a small piece of this thin skin.

Red Flint: A very hard fine-grained quartz mineral used for striking sparks from iron (red is an uncommon colour).

Red Path: The Red Path links The Creator to Man. The Black Path represents the teachings or stepping-stones to find truth and honesty on the meandering path of life. The paths are depicted as zig-zag patterns in art, decoration and pictographs.

Smoke-tanned Moose Hide: Moose hide that is cured in a traditional Aboriginal (First Nations) method that includes softening the hide with animal brains and smoking it over a slow fire.

Smudge: A prayer ceremony in which the smoke of one or more smoldering Sacred Medicines: Sweet Grass, Prairie Sage, Eastern White Cedar is wafted with a fan or feather, or with one's hands, over a person to cleanse and purify the mind, body and spirit. The smoke is drawn by hand to one's heart. Smudges also may be used to purify other items.

Spirit-seed Beads: In many cultures throughout the World, tiny beads of seeds or other materials are worn to embody the spirits of ancestors through prayer.

"Story Necklace": A necklace made of many objects that tells a spiritual or real-life story. Such a necklace might include animal teeth, quills, claws, bones, fish scales and beads of pearls, shells, seeds, metal, wood or stone.

"Strike-a-light" Bag: A small bag that contains fire making supplies: flint and iron to strike sparks, tinder and punk.

Sweetgrass: The imaginary old Medicine Woman in this story received her Spirit Name from her Elder in prayer to The Creator in a naming ceremony. The name *Sweetgrass* is from the sacred plant, Sweet Grass or "Holy Grass". Aboriginal (First Nations) people use Sweet Grass smoke for cleansing in ceremonial prayers to The Creator. The three strands of a braid of Sweet Grass (also called Mother Earth's Hair) represent the human mind, body and spirit as well as the elements of Earth, Water and Fire. The knotted end holds the most power for times of great need.

Tree of Life: In Aboriginal (First Nations) culture, the flowering "Tree of Life" is the centre of The Creator. It extends its branches outward to breathe in life through its leaves. The roots are sent into the depths of Mother Earth to drink her nourishment. All of creation is interdependent and equal in the cycle of life and each part must be respected and shared for all to survive. The greatest gift from The Creator is LIFE.

V-formation: Lines of ducks or geese flying in a V-shaped group to take advantage of reduced resistance to airflow.

Vamps: The part of a moccasin that covers the top part of the foot.

White Birch Punk: Dried, rotted birch wood fibres used with tinder for starting fires.

White Planets: The two white planets in the solar system are Mercury, the small planet nearest to the Sun and Venus, the second planet, which often is referred to as the "Morning Star" or "Evening Star".

Worker-bees: The caste of honey bees that builds combs, gathers nectar, guards the Queen, protects the hive and feeds the larval bees.

Book Production

Prepress design and layout: Sharon Williams Franzin and William G. Franzin
Word and image processing: William G. Franzin
Original photographic images: Firmin G. Michiels
Paper stock: Text pages; 100 lb. Garda Silk White, 4 process colour
      Endsheets; 100 lb. Offset White, Metallic PMS Gold
      Hard cover; Rainbow over 100 pt. cover board, board in spine, gold foil stamped on spine and front cover
      Dust jacket; 100 lb. C1S, 4 process colour, 1/2-mil matte plastic lamination
Bindery: Sewn

Laughing Water Arts